★ TEDDY ★ BEAR
Treasury
VOLUME II

A Salute to Teddy

Identification & Values

Ken Yenke

★ ❦ ★

COLLECTOR BOOKS
A Division of Schroeder Publishing Co., Inc.

FRONT COVER: 17" Ideal Teddy, 1907; 13" Ideal Teddy, 1907; 15" Roulette Decamp Drummer, 1875.

BACK COVER: 16" Farnell, 1920 (teal blue).

Cover design by Beth Summers

Book design by Heather Warren

COLLECTOR BOOKS
P.O. Box 3009
Paducah, Kentucky 42002-3009

www.collectorbooks.com

Copyright © 2003 Ken Yenke

The current values in this book should be used only as a guide. They are not intended to set prices, which vary from one section of the country to another. Auction prices as well as dealer prices vary greatly and are affected by condition as well as demand. Neither the author nor the publisher assumes responsibility for any losses that might be incurred as a result of consulting this guide.

Searching For A Publisher?

We are always looking for people knowledgeable within their fields. If you feel that there is a real need for a book on your collectible subject and have a large comprehensive collection, contact Collector Books.

Contents

Dedication

A Salute To Teddy is a genuine "salute" to both the teddy bear, and to his namesake, Teddy Roosevelt. Teddy was a moral American who profoundly impacted the success of the best toy ever made…teddy's bear.

A very special thank you to Dave Coleman, our personal photographer. After Brenda and I pose the teddy bears, Dave always gets them to "say cheese" at just the right moment. Thanks for your friendship and assistance.

To those friends who are featured in Chapter Six, thank you for sending the photographs. A special thank you to Jeanne Behner who provided me with many original old photographs.

About the Author

Many wonderful things have happened since the release of *Teddy Bear Treasury* two years ago. Brenda and I will have been married 36 years this July…I mean 37 years this June!! We now have eight grandchildren, and everyone is in good health.

In 2001, I began writing a general antique column for the 25 Sun newspapers in the Cleveland, Ohio area, cleverly titled "Yenke Peddler." What a joy it has been, and the great reader response, including photos of teddy bears and other collectibles, fuels the creative mental fires.

This being a 100-year celebration of Roosevelt's teddy bear incident, American Greeting Cards Company is releasing fantastic teddy bear items for 2002. Over a dozen of our favorite teddy bears will be featured on these items.

Through television, radio, and various publications we are fortunate to continually make new collecting friends. Most important, our efforts have helped us retain all of our "good old friends." God bless America…and your families.

Ken Yenke

Foreword
An unsolicited letter from a Teddy Bear Treasury reader

Dear Ken,

I was unexpectedly hospitalized for a week (I am out now and did not need surgery, just some medical observation). Your book, *Teddy Bear Treasury*, really kept me from going stir-crazy, so the timing of its arrival to me was absolutely perfect!

I also want to commend you for the special photographs that are in the book. I have much admired but not developed a passion for antique bears. Many other books have helped inform me, but none stirred my deep emotions.

However, almost every photo in your book was totally charming. It conveyed the special appeal of each bear, and I found myself falling in love with every page.

I could never afford the bears, but the book is truly magical and will hold a special place in my personal library. Thank you so much! I look forward to more of your books in the future.

Shelia

PS. Bing, Schuco, Farnell…yes Ken, I feel the passion for bears truly blossoming now!

Author's note: As anyone who has ever written an article, or a book knows, the ultimate satisfaction comes from the realization that you have actually touched the heartstrings of the reader. Thank you, Shelia, for sharing the good you found in Teddy Bear Treasury.

Introduction

This book is intended as an entertaining guide and continuation of the first *Teddy Bear Treasury*. What fun Brenda and I had revisiting all the special friends in our collection. Our goal was to select only those bears that did not appear in the first book. If you see an item again, we are showing you the original owner's photo.

You are soon to be introduced to a whole new cast of original antique teddys and their friends. Within these pages, I have tried to pass on some of the original flavor of the early 1900s. You'll meet "Bear and Forbear," Smithsonian's twin, and see Then and Now photographs, and hopefully through this volume the lives of all these original plush toys will continue.

Chapter One
Free Appraisal...Know How Much Your Teddy Is Worth!

Thomas Jefferson, in a letter to John Adams in 1817, wrote the following about antiques. "A Morsel of Genuine History is a Thing So Rare as to be Always Valuable."

Many collectors have found us by way of *Teddy Bear Treasury*, requesting appraisals, evaluations, and general information on care and collecting. Just how valuable is your "Morsel of Genuine History?" Original teddy bears and other stuffed toys from the turn of the century have become very desirable, and in many cases the value has risen dramatically.

We shall begin this book the way we ended the last one, with a gift for you. I will gladly fill out an Evaluation Certificate (from page 158) for you, since you now own a copy of my book. Simply send me a photo of your teddy or animal, with a self-addressed stamped envelope. Include a copy of the certificate, and I will promptly send you an evaluation of your item. If you have more than one item, a nominal fee would be charged. Please e-mail me at kenyenke@aol.com, or send your questions to my post office box.

Allow me to tell you one of the many experiences I have had which substantiates the importance of reading books and studying photographs. I am frequently asked about my personal entry into the world of antique teddy bears. Many years ago, Brenda and I spotted an old teddy bear on the shelf of an antique store in Medina, Ohio. Although Brenda had collected a few bears, we did not have a really old one, aside from my childhood teddy, Snowcrop, from the 1950s.

The teddy we liked was a 1907 Steiff, I was told, and it would cost about $1,000.00. That price, way back then, was too high for the moment, so we would wait. By chance, about a week later, on our way back from a trip to southern Ohio, we happened upon a little shop's sign which read: "Closing Our Doors, and Moving Back East." I pulled up to the door and quickly found my way into the shop.

I walked through the store which specialized in 1950s memorabilia, and just as I was about to leave, I spotted a bushel basket full of plush animals behind the door. Familiar characters looked out from the basket: Winnie, Snoopy, and a very peculiar looking parrot. I lifted him from the basket, making note of his beautiful mohair colors. The most unique thing was a green mohair tail, which caused the parrot's head to go up and down when I moved it.

How much for the parrot, I asked? "Seven dollars and fifty cents", said the shop owner. "I am selling everything at cost today." He said he had purchased the whole basket of plush from a house sale years earlier, for less than $20.00. I paid the price and wished him a safe trip back east.

Why did I buy the parrot? I love books and had just finished reading about early twentieth century toys, namely from the Schuco Company of Germany. They described a mechanism that was located in the tail area. They mentioned that it made the animal say yes or no depending on how you moved the tail. I was hoping this was one of those 1920s toys.

The next week we headed for the Medina antique shop where the antique teddy was still on the shelf. True ending: The knowledgeable shop owner loved parrots and recognized this one as a Schuco. She gave me the antique teddy bear ($1,000.00 value then) and also $100.00 in cash for the exchange. Knowledge really did pay for our first antique teddy bear. By the way, the photo on the bottom of page 18 shows that bear. As I became more knowledgeable I discovered the bear was not a 1907 Steiff, but a 1907 Bruin. I don't care, we still have the bear and the love of reading good collector books.

Chapter Two
American & Political Bears

The longer I collect, the more enamored I become with the beginnings of these delightful stuffed friends. Included in this chapter are many of the "original" teddy bears with their owners. As you will notice throughout this and succeeding chapters, Brenda and I consider ourselves caretakers of these wonderful items. Oftentimes, the reason we were given the chance to purchase was to see that the life of a particular teddy would begin anew. True to our promise to the original owners or their relatives, within these pages we are reintroducing many teddy bears, animals, and rare photographs. Until now, only the original owners have enjoyed their company.

Won't You Be My Teddy Bear Pin, circa 1907, $150.00; Roosevelt Bears trading card, circa 1907, uncirculated, $75.00; About Our Candidate, 1904 miniature book about Teddy's life. $200.00.

An original campaign pin from 1900, McKinley for President, Teddy Roosevelt for Vice President. $75.00.

President Theodore "Teddy" Roosevelt, 1907.

Olive Fell's 1920 drawing of a bear cub, titled "Wishing." This looks very much like the Clifford Berryman cub from the 1902 hunting incident.

Dating from 1936, this is a rare placecard drawn by Clifford Berryman for the Arts Club meeting on January 16, of that year. Teddy's bear is still ever-present even though this was done 34 years after the hunting event. 4" by 7" in mint condition. $200.00.

Dating from March 13, 1947, this Arts Club Dinner drawing was perhaps Clifford Berryman's final rendition of the famed bear cub. Berryman died in 1949. 4" by 7" in mint condition. $200.00.

One of the many colorful tunes that were inspired by the Teddy bear. $75.00.

One of my favorite prints from the 1907 Judge Magazine. Titled "Uncle Sam Unmasked," under it is none other than our patriotic friend, Theodore "Teddy" Roosevelt. Circa 1907. $50.00.

Measuring 5" tall, this leather penwipe says "One of the Bears Teddy Didn't Get." With felt backing, this rare piece is valued at $150.00.

This 4-foot-tall tree stump was transformed into a great-looking bear cub by a local carver. $400.00.

17" Ideal Teddy with rust-colored yarn nose and claws. In near mint condition from the original owner, value is $3,500.00.

Roosevelt's silhouette from 1910. $250.00. Next is my all-time favorite teddy photo. This is an actual schoolhouse photo from 1908. Measuring 11" by 13", this is truly a salute to the 50th birthday of Teddy Roosevelt, who was born on October 27th, 1858. $500.00+.

A closer look shows that the girls have brought their Teddy bears, and the boys are dressed like Teddy Roosevelt, the bear hunter. This photo is actually dated October 27, 1908. Notice the looks, dress, and demeanor of these early twentieth century students. Let's get a closer look, and identify the teddy bears.

Let's begin with the white Steiff on the end, then move to the Bear-Doll by Baker & Bigler. An early Ideal is next, then a cinnamon-colored Steiff, and a light-colored homemade teddy is next. The last teddy shown is a golden mohair Steiff. Happy 50th, President Roosevelt!

Moosy is a Steiff from the 1950s. Mint with all identification, he is valued at $500.00. Teddy's 1904 campaign pin is perfect and valued at $100.00.

As we look at the profile of this Bull Moose, we can reflect on his significance to Teddy Roosevelt. In 1912, this was the symbol of the Bull Moose Party, and Teddy was their candidate. He defeated William Howard Taft, but lost to Woodrow Wilson.

The Jilted Dolly & the Teddy Bear.

Dolly gets an Insiration.

BILLIE GETS BUSY.

"The Jilted Dolly and the Teddy Bear." The Teddy Bear quickly became the toy of choice for girls as well. By 1907, stories like this one became quite prevalent. Nearly 100 years later, Teddys and dolls are getting along much better, thank you. Value is $150.00 for the six card set.

214

Copyright 1907
By Bamforth & Co.

CAPTAIN BABY BUNTING
(Rocking Horse Brigade)

Dear Little Baby Bunting, Mamma's darling, four years old,
Sat on his Rocking Horsey, like a soldier brave and bold,
Mamma and Baby's sweetheart, pretty little blue eyed Miss,
Hear him say I'm off to Battle, Mamma says "Good-bye" with tender kiss.

Captain Baby Bunting of the Rocking Horse Brigade,
At home your mother's waiting, with a pretty little, witty blue eyed maid,
Little soldier, when you're older, may the Glory never fade,
From Captain Baby Bunting of the Rocking Horse Brigade.

"Song Copyrighted 1906 by Helf & Hager Co., Publishers,
43 West 28th St. N. Y.

Captain Baby Bunting photo card is dated 1907. A close-up allows us to see the dog and teddy face-to-face. The verse was published in 1906. $50.00.

This 17" tall Aetna teddy bear is one of the most highly sought American Bears. This original specimen with shoe button eyes is among their earliest. $3,000.00.

A side view gives an opportunity to gauge the claw formation, head design, and side-placed ears.

A very primitive American black teddy, from 1910. Standing 16" tall, he has wire rod joints and glass eyes. $2,000.00.

Another look at this sweet black mohair teddy. This color in early teddys is rare indeed.

"I pledge allegiance to the flag," says this little puppet from 1940. Composition head and cloth body. $50.00.

This original 1½" tall mug from 1907 holds a blue jointed plush bear from 1930. Mug, $75.00. The little bear holds a birthday candle. $125.00.

Here is the same little girl, a little older, with her American Bruin teddy.

A Christmas photo from 1907. Notice the tree of toys, beside which she holds her American Bruin teddy.

American Bruin teddy today, nearly 95 years later. As shown $1,500.00. (This is the first Antique Teddy we acquired many years ago.)

Knickerbocker made some of the most beautiful teddy bears. This hard-to-find 10" white version dates from the 1930s and is in mint condition. $750.00.

A sweet American Character Teddy in the hard-to-find 8" size, dating from 1930, $150.00; seated with him is a 3" brown miniature Petz Teddy from the same period. $100.00.

This front view shows the distinctive look of Miller's teddys. On page 69 of *Teddy Bear Treasury, Volume I*, you will find his 20" companion.

Miller Mfg. advertised the antiseptic teddy in 1907. This 10" version is one of the hardest to locate by collectors, In mint condition, it is valued at $2,000.00. The 1907 Teddy Roosevelt metal bookmark is valued at $150.00.

Ideal's 17" version of this same teddy at left. In magnificent condition, obtained from the original owner, unfortunately there were no early photos of her with the bear. With provenance, $3,500.00+

Ideal teddy bears are among the oldest American versions. What a pleasure to find an original owner, then and now. I obtained this 12" Ideal from the original owner's daughter. The photo is from 1907, the bear stands behind it today. With photo, $3,000.00.

Another view of this great little teddy and the photo of his original owner some 95 years ago.

Ideal's cinnamon bear is proudly held by the smaller of these brothers in a candid 1907 photo. What a great photograph!

What a splendid Christmas greeting from 1907. This American card displays a little girl with her Ideal teddy and a lamb on wheels. Card, $25.00.

Ideal's cinnamon bear today. $2,000.00+

Another view of this sweet Ideal cinnamon teddy, some 95 years later than the first photo.

The little girl in the center is the second-generation owner of the Ideal teddy shown. The photo dates from 1930.

The bear in the 1930 photo is shown here with a cotton rabbit that has companioned the teddy since 1907. The Teddy with photo and rabbit, $3,000.00+.

A girl's smile is captured in this 1907 photo. The Ideal teddy looks splendid…then…and now!

A current photo shows this same teddy, nearly 95 years later. With photo, $4,000.00.

Another glance at this great personality!

An 11" Ideal teddy displays his "mousy" look. What a great bear, in mint condition from 1909. $2,000.00.

Ideal's white mohair muff is highly treasured. This one, from 1908, is in great condition. As we know, these were made to interest the little girls of that time in Teddy bear mania. $2,500.00.

Sitting above the white Ideal muff is a dark cinnamon version from 1907. American made with shoe button eyes, the smaller size is very rare. In perfect condition, $2,500.00.

Early American teddy bears are even more attractive when they are wearing their original sweaters! This pre-1910 teddy is 12" tall and valued at $1,200.00. The sweater is original, valued at $250.00.

These photos capture the years 1909 through 1925 and the growth of the teddy bear's original owner over that period. A great study, and the bear is a 25" dark brown American teddy. Wish I had a photo of the teddy today. Three photos, $100.00.

A boy and his bear, photographed in 1910. The bear is a 20" Ideal of that vintage. $25.00.

Sisters share the spotlight with two American teddy bears and two German bisque dolls. The photo was taken in 1908. $35.00.

This 1907 photo shows a little girl and her American teddy. $25.00.

Lazy days of summer 1910 provide the perfect setting for this little boy and his line-up of playthings. Closest to him is an Ideal teddy from that year. $25.00.

Baseball 1907...a store display from the Marks Rothenberg Store shows a teddy bear baseball game in progress, Texas A&M versus the University of Mississippi. The teddy bears are from an unidentified mixture of makers. Great early photo. $100.00.

The top right photo on page 20 shows an Ideal teddy very similar to the one shown in these 1910 pictures. I believe the dog is a Bing. $40.00.

The American dog is looking at a little Schuco humanized crow, made in the 1950s. Crow, $175.00.

Selling for $1.25 in 1948, this little dog was sold to raise money for the Japanese War Widows Association. It was made and tagged in the United States. $125.00.

Magnificent! This is a 1920s hand-carved chocolate box by the Quimby Chocolate Company of California. The bear is carved from California redwood and sits snuggly atop his hollow log container. On page 114 of *Teddy Bear Treasury* I you can find another version of this 1920s candy box. Excellent condition, $750.00.

The joys of sharing cannot be expressed often enough. American Greeting Cards brought our 1930s Atlanta Playthings Company teddy out for a special Valentine card last year.

The set dates from 1950, but it says in its literature that its idea goes back into the 1800s. The simple idea of the set is to use the bears to communicate with your spouse. By rotating the bears either toward or away from the other, you indicate your feelings of that moment. Never go to sleep until both bears face forward, hand in hand. You may have noticed the terms "Bear" and "Forbear" on many of the original teddy bear postcards as well as in early teddy bear children's books. This rare set in "unused" condition, $350.00.

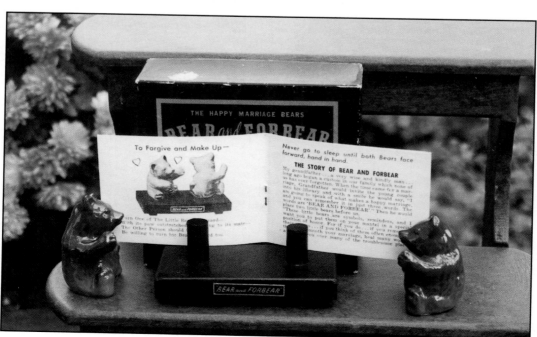

The Uncle Remus teddys were made for only two years, 1906 and 1907. Joel Chandler Harris, author of the Uncle Remus stories, died in 1908, and it seems none of these bears were marketed after that.

Uncle Remus is one of the earliest and rarest makers of American teddy bears. Our 20" shown here is displaying his voice box. Inside the black tape we found it lined with a New York Times news section, dated 1906.

Standing at the window, we can appreciate the long arms and dynamic profile of this prize teddy bear. They were designed to look as much like imported Steiff teddy bears as possible.

The exclusive feature of Uncle Remus bears is the way their eyes were fastened. They routed them down to the neck joint and then up and out of the back of the head. When you find an Uncle Remus bear, the eyes are always deep-set and tight as a drum. Excellent condition, $5,000.00+.

Chapter Three

Bing Bears

Many of you know of my fondness for the original Bing teddy bears, as well as any of Bing's countless toys. Having written a definitive book on Bing, my research served to enamor me even more with this company and their history. They were the largest toy producer in the world from 1905 until 1932, employing as many as 7,000 workers at one time.

Bing toys' and teddys' values have skyrocketed over the past several years. Study this chapter closely, and perhaps you will be able to spot a special Bing item at a flea market or antique show. Good luck!

Bing was one of the most prolific toy manufacturers of all time. The original company, Gerbruder Bing, lasted from 1865 until 1932, manufacturing a limitless variety of toys. From trains to teddys, treasures from these early years are currently being sought by collectors around the world.

This photo is from the 1906 Bing toy catalog. Notice the train and three animals.

An elephant, lion, and bear are the original pieces for this set. The animals are felt, with sewn bead eyes, just like those from the Steiff Company. The train is definitely made by Bing, and the set as shown is valued at $3,000.00.

The back of the 1906 train today, showing the GBN (Gerbruder Bing Nuremberg) logo. The 3" felt bear from the actual train sits atop.

The Hagenbeck Menagerie is advertised on this side of the train car. Carl Hagenbeck's trained circus appeared at the Columbia World's Fair in 1893. This remarkable stenciled car with its animals is a treasure.

Dynamic duo! Sitting wearing the green bow is a very limited reproduction of our original 1907 Bing teddy bear named Austin. Linda Fullmer, friend and artist extraordinaire, capably re-created our original for a few lucky collectors. Replica, $600.00. Original, $15,000.00+.

Bing's original bear on wheels is shown here. This 8" long cinnamon mohair bear is absolutely mint. Standing on iron Marklin wheels, he has his original collar and linked pull chain. I obtained him from the original owner's family, and what a treat to have a Christmas photo from 1910 with this little bear featured!

Taken outside, for better lighting, this is the original 1910 Christmas photo of the Bing bear with his new owner.

Here is the little 8" Bing today...he was preserved in a shoe box for 90 years. This is his photo taken outside 91 years later!

In this photo we can see the shadow of the picture-taker as she photographs this great scene. An enlargement gives us a slightly better view of the Bing bear on wheels. With provenance, $4,000.00.

A study in the features of Bing bears on wheels. The 20" long "grizzly" by Bing has glass eyes and a horizontally stitched nose. He has a push voice under his tummy. The leather collar and chain are exactly the same as the smaller Bing's. The larger Bing was made in 1918, and carries a red BW tag on his leg. The smaller bear with shoe button eyes and a vertically sewn nose hails from the pre-1912 era. The larger bear is valued at $3,500.00 and is in excellent condition.

Observe the great face. Bings originally were designed from life, so realism was paramount.

A pair of great Bing bear faces. Large bear 1918, smaller bear 1910.

Bing shows another special bear on wheels in the 12" size. Although in mint condition, he does not have the standard leather collar and chain. He dates from 1918 and is valued at $2,500.00.

Sharing the spot with our Bing bear is a German mache rabbit with a worsted wool body dating from 1900. If you move his wire tail, his ears will move back and forth.

In this photo you can detect the small wire by the rabbit's tail. Honey can from 1900, $150.00; bunny with moveable ears, $250.00.

A final look at the 12" Bing on wheels will introduce you to the smallest Bing on wheels. Measuring about 6", he dates from 1918, and has glass eyes. This little bear has wooden wheels and has been played with more than his companion bears. Small bear, $1,000.00.

Bing's original walking bear from 1907 is shown in this winter photo. Standing 8" tall, this key-wind clockwork toy is actually a skater.

A close-up of his face shows the metal GBN ear tag, his tiny shoe button eyes, and the meticulously sewn horizontally stitched nose.

A couple of early Bing features can be seen on these standing walking bears. Notice the GBN metal tag in this bear's ear, which marks it as one of their earliest productions. The head and body are one-piece construction, peanut shell shaped, without a jointed head. This rare skater in working condition, $5,000.00.

Transition time is captured here, from skating bear to skating teddy. The dressed Bing was first made in 1908. He has a jointed head and a teddy bear face. $5,000.00+.

Bing's skaters/walkers from 1908 through 1920 are some of the most charming toys ever produced.

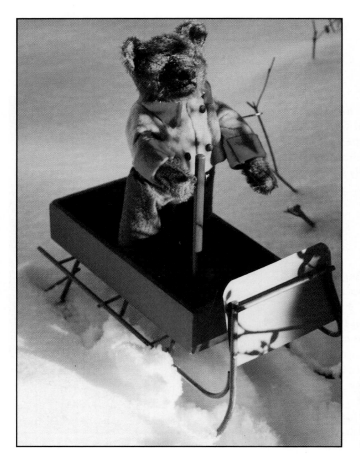

Notice the natural look of this sweet cinnamon Bing Skater. The metal skates are attached by clips to his feet. The red BW tag on his arm is the 1918 Bing identification mark. He is in great working condition...nearly 90 years old.

A Closer Look...

Bing's genius is displayed with their jumping frog shown here. From their 1908 catalog, this 8" long felt frog carries a wood and velvet cat-tail as he merrily jumps along. This frog has the red BW metal tag on his arm, which means he was sold after 1918, but I believe he was made closer to 1910. His top hat is a push squeaker, and the clockwork mechanism is wound from his stomach area. The Bing frog complete with cat-tail, excellent condition, extremely rare, $2,000.00.

Two Little Bears **from 1907 features some of the most colorful prints. Our 1912 Bing walker has more than a passing interest in our little performers. Book, $125.00.**

Proudly pausing at the bench, this 8" tall Bing teddy toy has quite a stoic look. In great overall condition, $5,000.00.

How sweet can a face be? This smallish Trippel-Trappel terrier dates from 1908, and is in mint condition. Measuring 8" from head to toe, $500.00+.

Original photo of a little girl in 1908, with her Bing Trippel-Trappel walking dog. I received the original dog and a bear from this family.

The dog in the photo and the original 1908 box. Value with provenance, $1,500.00+.

More of this great dog and his original box. Measures 10" from head to tail.

A better view of the dog when brand new in 1908.

With dog sitting up, we can see the special metal wheels that allow this dog to emulate walking when pulled.

A final look at the 10" terrier and an introduction to his smaller friend who measures 8" from head to tail. Pug with original tag, in mint condition, $750.00+.

Bing's 1908 Trippel-Trappel walking sheep, mint in the box. Although dogs were the most commonly produced walkers, this rare sheep has all the personality of the best of their pooches. With original box, $2,000.00.

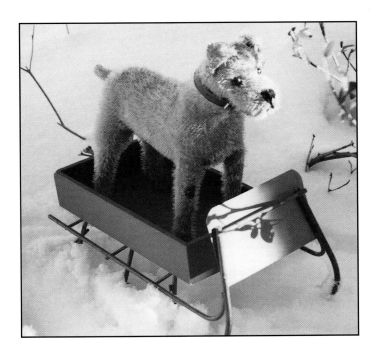

Bing produced very few dogs, so this terrier is especially nice to view. Notice the bluish metal tag on his leg which indicates he was manufactured in the 1920s. In excellent condition, $500.00+.

The terrier has nearly all the original mohair, but the pile is short and rather sparse. With original collar, shoe button eyes, and identification tag, he is a very special dog.

Bing's terrier is enjoying the sounds of the Bing Kiddyphone from 1920.

Lithographed scenes enhance this great sounding toy record player. Key-wind clockwork is one of Bing's original areas of specialization.

Both of these Bing items were made about the same time. The child's record player is one of four models made by Bing. The graphics are all wonderfully done.

A view from this side shows a dancing bear, performing to the sounds of the minstrel.

In great working condition, this desirable style of the 1920s Bing Kiddyphone is valued up to $1,000.00.

Bing chimpanzees have great personalities. Shown here are two different styles. The store-new chimp on the tricycle was made in 1925. When pulled, he pedals along in a dapper fashion. The chimp on the bench is a clockwork jumper. Wind the key, and he will jump realistically across any floor or table. He dates from 1908, and is valued at $1,500.00+. Tricycle chimp, $1,000.00.

What is better than one Bing chimpanzee? Two of them hanging from a tree! These fellows are from 1908 and 1918.

The chimp on the top of the ladder has the red BW tag on his arm, a new identification mark used after 1918. The chimp under the ladder is about 10 years older.

Our parting shot of this chimp is a close-up to allow you a better study of the great facial features of the Bing chimp.

Bing teddys have always enchanted me. Look at this 17" beauty from the 1925-1930 era. What a face!

His profile stance allows us to notice the little Schuco bear head pin on his scarf. It is an original adornment from the 1920s. Bing bear, $2,500.00+. Schuco head pin, $250.00.

Original photo of a boy and his 1908 Bing teddy bear. The next photo is of the 1908 bear today.

Bing's 12" teddy from 1908, in excellent condition. Teddy with provenance, $4,500.00+

The original Bing from the above photo, sitting with teddy's best friend.

Bing's fabulous white mohair teddy bear from 1912, 16" tall. $5,000.00+.

"Dynamic duo" describes these white mohair Bing teddy bears, 16" and 14" versions of the very desirable white teddy. In wonderful condition, $5,000.00 and $4,000.00, respectively.

It is amazing what a 2" difference in a teddy's height can make to his overall appearance. Notice in this picture that the 14" bear has a horizontally stitched nose and the 16" bear has a vertically stitched nose. The color of the nose and claws was only used on their white mohair pieces.

Considered rare, these two Bings date from around 1912.

The outdoor photos of our rare pair lend a richness to their special personalities.

I hope you're not seeing too many pictures of this beauty...this is the first time he was ever photographed for a book...and he loves it.

A final look at the rare white 14" Bing teddy from 1912.

These long-nosed Bings are 12" tall and are among the tip-toe style patterns made from 1912 through 1920. Also called "sentry styled" because of their meer-cat pose when standing. Rare, $4,000.00 each.

These mint Bings have tilt-forward growlers which are the typical style for all of this maker's bears.

This long-haired Bing measures 14" tall and possesses that special "profile."
In mint condition, $5,000.00.

Bing's largest stock sized teddy bear is shown here in profile. This gentle giant is 40" tall.

Standing tall at the patio door, he awaits the first cleaning in his 85-year life.

Cleaned and brushed, our 40" Bing sits proudly with his little 8" Bing skating bear.

Named "St. Valentine," since he was a gift to Brenda on that day, he is shown basking in the afternoon sunshine. He has a loud tilt-forward growler, which matches his 40" size.

Just for perspective, see how large he is in my arms.

St. Valentine, because of his size, condition, and desirable rarity, $15,000.00+.

His side view shows how thick and rich his mohair is. Although we generally collect bears that are 20" or less, this guy was an easy exception to make!

Close-up of the BW tag.

Bing's white teddys welcome a rare newcomer.

Standing behind the 16" white Bing is a
16" cinnamon-red Bing from 1925.

This picture allows you to compare the noses on bears which
date from 1925 and 1912, respectively. Notice the blue BW tag on
the cinnamon bear's arm.

Notice the richness of color and pile on this
1925 Bing beauty as he rests on the bench.

Obtained from an original owner, this 16" Bing is one of the most unusual specimens I have ever seen. It has such a real look and the sweetness of a favorite puppy.

The final profile photo gives more perspective on the stature of this remarkable Bing, one of our favorite teddy bears. Near mint with identification, $7,500.00+.

Bing produced a wonderful look in the 1920 era. This 20" example is in mint condition, with a tilt-forward growler. He is typical of the honey-colored Bing teddy bears of that period. $4,000.00+

This miniature dresser is an original turn-of-the-century FAO Schwarz toy. Underneath is an ivory-colored celluloid plate which reads: MANUFACTURED FOR FAO SCHWARZ TOYS, FIFTH AVENUE AND THIRTY FIRST STREET, NEW YORK. It measures 18" tall by 24" long.

As he stands atop the FAO Schwarz toy dresser, the 1925, 14" Bing teddy sees the card is pre-1900.

The address is 12 East 14th St., Union Square, N.Y., different from that under the dresser.

Look what Teddy found in the dresser...an original miniature mohair coat and hat which fit perfectly. Teddy, $2,500.00+; mini-coat and hat, $200.00; FAO toy dresser, $500.00; Christmas card, $75.00.

Bing's pull-bear on wheels was a universal favorite. Dating from 1900, complete, $2,000.00+.

A 1915 celluloid Uncle Sam, standing 8" tall, $100.00+. The 1907 black and white print in an original teddy bear frame (see the two at the bottom), $200.00.

"Big" Bings emit strong characters. This 24" teddy from 1912 displays the elongated nose that Bings have become known for. $7,500.00.

The eyes are the windows of a very soulful bear. Even with the thinning mohair, he is a treasure.

"Rat-a-tat-tat" goes the drum. An original 13" 1907 Bing teddy, with the rare tin GBN arrow in the ear, sits across from his 8" companion Bing from 1912.

As our two Bings "say cheese," we can check their value. $6,000.00+ for the 13" with tag in ear, and 2,000.00 for the little white Bing.

A 16" Bing cinnamon-brown teddy from 1915, and a rare white cat puppet by Bing from 1920, with a blue BW id tag on her arm. This is a great photo! Bear, $5,000.00. Cat puppet, $750.00.

What stories are these two special Bings sharing?

The cat is supposed to be stuck in the tree, but instead it is Mr. Cinnamon Bear.

Bing's rare cat puppet displays a sweet look that all plush lovers appreciate. The windmill is from Bing's train accessories, dating from 1920, $150.00.

What a bear! The water tower is part of Bing's train accessories from the 1920 era. $150.00.

I don't want to overdo this, but I want to show a couple more pictures of these guys. They are great!

What a surprise! This is an original 5" tall "teddy's bear." Dating from 1904, this white wool bear was stored for nearly 90 years after Teddy Roosevelt's election in 1904. $1,000.00+.

Standing, our cinnamon Bing wants to see what is in this turn of the 20th century furrier box.

A parting glance from Mr. Cinnamon. Heinrich Mueller used a design very similar to this Bing's in 1920 when he made his first yes-no bears under the name of Schuco.

Chapter Four

English, French, and German Bears

English teddys have a personality unlike any other. Usually the mohair is the very best, and once in a while you capture a special "antique" look that rivals any other make. Farnell has captured this look often. Enjoy that look.

French bears are among the earliest, especially in the mechanical area. You are about to see some of the rarest and best kept secrets in the teddy bear's development. I am forever entranced with their performances.

German-made varieties are endless. I have selected several special items to give you a taste of the dramatic workmanship present in these early teddys and animals.

English Bears

Hot water bottle bears, especially this rubber type, are quite rare. This English version was made in 1907 by the Duncan Company. It measures 12" tall and is in excellent condition, having been properly stored. $300.00.

Farnell teddy bears are among my very favorite. This 12" Farnell dates from around 1910, and is in near mint condition. His companion is a Farnell lamb with the original tag on its underside. The little primitive looking lamb dates from 1920-1930. Teddy, $3,000.00. Lamb, $150.00.

Another companion for the 12" Farnell. Shown here is an original bear on all fours, with a Farnell tag on his underside. Although not jointed, his great condition and rarity from the 1920 era give him a value of $350.00.

Sitting outside, this magnificent 12" Farnell has all the personality of a bear twice his size!

Pandas are becoming more popular with collectors. The two shown are early favorites, dating from 1930 and 1940. Standing is a yes-no Schuco panda in the 12" size. Sitting on the bench is a great English panda from the 1930s, made by Chiltern. Both pandas are in excellent condition. Schuco's panda, $2,000.00. Chiltern's panda, $750.00.

Farnell made some of the sweetest looking bears, as we see here. This little 10" dates from the 1930s, and is near mint condition. His squeaker is great and his mohair very thick and long. $500.00+.

Chiltern made some great teddy bears. This one is among my all-time favorites, named Ting-a-ling. When you pick him up and gently shake him, you here the ting-a-ling of the bells encased in his tummy. He is made with a similar look to the original Steiff closed mouth teddy baby of the 1930s. This fellow stands on his flat-finished felt feet. Near mint condition, 20" tall, $1,000.00+.

What a face and what a story this turquoise teddy could tell. He was found wrapped in a brown paper bag that had been placed in the back of a closet nearly 75 years ago. Teal? Aqua? Turquoise? Whatever the shade, he is in mint, unplayed-with condition. Standing 16" tall, he is indeed a plump teddy.

This rare, 16" tissue-mint 1920 Farnell teddy steps outside for the first time in 75 years, to give his "Salute to Teddy."

An excellent look at teddy's profile and coloration. The antique sled with green and teal flowers painted on its side seems to have been made for teddy.

Look closely at the pearl cotton cord used for his nose and signature webbed claws. The only tell-tale sign of aging on this Bruin is the slight deterioration of the brown paint inside the glass eyes. Losing the paint is very typical for the earliest Farnell teddys, so more often than not, they appear to have always had clear glass eyes.

When the owner brought this bear to me, Brenda opened the bag and fell in love with this teddy. Brenda's birthday is December 28, and the birthstone for December is turquoise, how appropriate! Today, after three quarters of a century stored in a brown paper bag...he is out of the closet! Happy birthday, Brenda. No value available.

French Bears

Fernand Martin's original plush toy bear. Keywound from the back, this 7" tall toy dances swiftly across a table. He has a metal head with light flossing applied, and a lightweight felt covers his mechanical body. This is the same style as shown in the 1907 print at right. This 110-year-old working toy bear is valued at $2,000.00+.

Besse Pease Guttman's 1907 print shows a child playing a flute while a bear dances. The bear in the photo is an 1880s walking bear made by the Fernand Martin Company. This bear does the "twist" as he lumbers forward from foot to foot. Print, $75.00.

Roullette Decamp made some of the earliest mechanical animals. The preferred covering on the finest realistic animals was rabbit fur. This is an original 1800s mechanical bear with his original wooden box. Standing 8" tall, when wound he will growl...open and close his mouth...turn his head left then right...go down to the ground on all fours...and then stand upright. In working condition with box, $3,000.00.

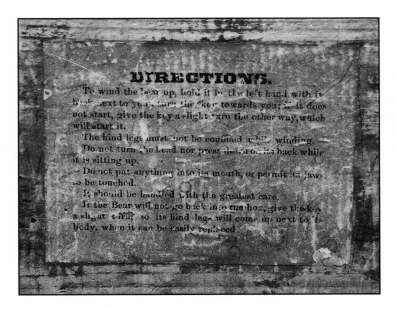

DIRECTIONS.

To wind the bear up, hold it in the left hand with its back next to you; turn the key towards you; if it does not start, give the key a slight turn the other way, which will start it.

The hind legs must not be confined while winding.

Do not turn the head nor press down on its back while it is sitting up.

Do not put anything into its mouth, or permit its jaw to be touched.

It should be handled with the greatest care.

If the Bear will not go back into the box, give the key a slight turn, so its hind legs will come up next to its body, when it can be easily replaced.

These directions are printed on the outside of the bear's original box. Although hard to read, it gives pointers like "don't put anything into the bear's mouth."

Made around 1875, 15" tall, and he's got rhythm!

Are you smiling? That is the first thing I did when I first looked at this remarkable bear. Roullette Decamp's clockwork wind-up allows this fellow to slowly tap out a rhythm, alternating from left to right paws. He is all original. I must thank my good friend Jim Buckey, who spent long hours in his machine shop freeing up the mechanism which works like a finely tuned clock. Photos of this bear being repaired appear in Chapter Seven.

71

The toy drum is perfect and original, from 1875, and the bear plays it ever so lightly.

This closer view of the wind-up bear shows the wooden paws, composition nose with an original wire muzzle attached, and clear glass eyes with black pupils.

A final glance at this great toy bear. In working condition, $3,000.00+.

Roullette Decamp created great mechanical bears. The two shown here are 10" tall and have clockwork mechanisms which are wound by turning their left arms. When you wind the arms around and release them, the bears will either do somersaults across the floor, or if hung by their hands from a wire, they will do high wire flips.

A closer view shows the composition nose, wooden paws, clear glass eyes, and dual-colored rabbit fur. In working condition, $1,500.00+ each.

German Bears

EDUCA, or Eduard Cramer was responsible for some of the best teddy bears ever made. In the center, I am intentionally showing you a replica of their Bearkin. It is so good, we had to put him among his original ancestors. On the left is a brassy-colored 10" from 1930. On the other side is a "wild" 11" teddy from the same period. These wonderful teddys are worth $2,500.00 each; the replica in the center, $175.00.

Barnhardt & Dorst mechanical bears were made before teddy bears but were continued after the introduction of teddys because of their unique play value. Shown in this photo are two great examples made in the early 1900s and distributed from Germany by the Barnhardt & Dorst Company. Acting like performing circus bears of their day, the light gold bear sounds the cymbals, while the dancing bear gently nods his head and right paw in approval. These bears are 6" tall, marked Germany on the bottom, and in mint condition. $750.00 each.

King Charles Spaniels are very expressive animals, and their toy counterparts are no less endearing. The dog on his right is a mechanical dog from an unknown German maker, dating from around 1920, and stands 7" tall. The black and white is a Steiff five-way jointed version from 1912. He is nearly 12" long.

When you wind this little spaniel, he gently waves his paws and gingerly turns around. Glass eyes, composition nose, and mohair over mache body make him very desirable. Near perfect condition, $1,500.00.

Clemens and Cramer are seated together in this photo. The open mouth on the Clemens gives him a special personality. What a great pair of bears from the 1930 and 1940s. Clemens' value, $500.00.

Do you like miniatures? These two little items are wonderful examples of how great smalls can be. The bunny is from Germany, circa 1900. Standing 3" high, made of velvet over papier-mache, he is valued at $200.00. The teddy is made by Eli of Germany and stands 3½" tall. His head is jointed, the arms are bendable, and he stands on metal feet. This 1930s gem is made of silk plush. This is the only one I have ever seen. In pristine condition, $900.00+.

Bright eyes! Outside, the 11" tall Cramer displays his long mohair. Typical of this maker, the eyes are clear glass painted brown with a black pupil.

A 6" cat from 1900 or so shows his original bell and ribbon. The body is mache with velvet, airbrushed. $250.00.

Both from Germany, the rabbit with the moveable ears (shown earlier) keeps company with the little Admiral Perry Eskimo or Teddy Doll. In mint condition, from 1909, this chubby little celluloid faced doll in like new condition, $500.00+.

Collectors seem to favor polar bears, and I am no exception. The bear in front with the tag is a 1950 Hermann polar bear with a great face enhanced by perfect airbrush touches. The angora white polar bear opposite him is made by Petz in the 1940s. $250.00+ each.

Don't miss this photo...sitting on bench is an original 1920s Jopi miniature jointed white teddy. Standing is a mint tipped mohair musical Jopi, 16" tall. When you squeeze his Swiss music box, he plays a heavenly tune. Little bear, $500.00; 16" bear, $3,000.00+.

This outdoors pose of the Jopi shows a little more of his personality. I wish you could hear the tune!

Jopi cats are shown with a tiny Steiff mouse looking on. These 9" tall musical cats are from the 1920s, valued at $1,000.00 each. The little mouse is valued at $125.00 and is from the 1950s.

(Left) Above the Jopi bear from 1920, stands a companion cat by the same maker. Remarkable is the fact that they play the same tune when their "glockenspiels" are squeezed. Rare indeed. Cat, $1,000.00+; bear, $3,000.00+.

There is a pinkish cast to this little teddy's mohair. She is a 9" tall Jopi, in perfect condition, dating from the 1930s. Rare size and special look give her a value of $900.00+.

Kersa is best known for its cats and puppets. This German company also made splendid teddy bears with distinct faces, as shown on this 12" example from 1950. White mohair in perfect condition, $1,200.00+.

Mutzli cornered the market on cute with these two examples from 1940. The tag in the ear was the earlier way of marking their bears, and later they moved the tag to the "heart." These 9" beauties are worth $500.00+ each.

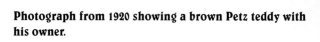

Photograph from 1920 showing a brown Petz teddy with his owner.

Petz teddy bear from 1940 with his milk glass identification pin. Hard to find 6" size teddy, $300.00.

Petz made this early example in 1912, and he is 19" tall when standing. Near mint condition, $1,000.00.

Schuco remains one of my favorite early toy and teddy makers. The first Teddy Bear Treasury features many styles from this prolific maker. The two shown here are in perfect condition and are the famed yes-no variety. When their tail is moved up and down, their heads bob "yes," and when the tail is moved right or left, the heads move to indicate "no." With the red US Zone tag on his chest is our 8" teddy, from 1948. The gold 12" mohair teddy is the original version of the yes-no teddy from around 1920. Notice the more stoic look generated from the original. The post-war bear was by design a little friendlier and more cub-like. Smaller bear, $1,000.00+; older gold bear from 1920, $2,000.00+.

In this photo you can see the tails on each bear, as well as their heads cocked upward and downward. These were truly the first mechanical "talking" bears, though non-verbal.

Schuco used this great yes-no mechanism in other animals as well as the teddy bears. Notice a very early cat and dog from the Schuco Company. The 6" tall cat has satin-lined ears and a tail that makes it move in the yes-no method. The cute long-haired dog also is a yes-no type. In wonderful condition, the cat is valued at $500.00, and the dog is valued at $750.00+. They both date from the 1930s.

Enjoy another view of this pair of Schuco yes-no toys.

Top: What kind of Schuco dog is this?
Middle: Notice how the dog's rear feet have moved closer to the front feet in this picture.
Bottom: The 8" yes-no teddy shown earlier is ready to take the Tip-Top dog for a walk.

When sitting up, the dog shows its wheeled feet. In 1912, Heinrich Mueller left Bing to start his own toy company, known as Schuco. Bing produced the Trippel-Trappel walking toys first in 1908; Schuco made a slight change to the original design and called their walkers Tip-Top. With the Schuco walkers, the front feet are stationary and the back feet move a couple of inches, then snap back in to produce a pushing force. Schuco Tip-Top animals are rare. $750.00+.

Strunz was one of the original mohair animal makers at the beginning of the twentieth century. This 10" long bear has two tiny wheels on his back feet. His nose is composition and has a chain attached to lead the bear around, just as circus trainers would have done a century ago. The body is mache with mohair covering. With very little wear, a realistic original Wilhelm Strunz toy bear like this is valued at $1,500.00+.

Shown in the original pre-1910 Strunz catalog is a "Pillow Bear." What a unique character, with his pillow-shaped body. He has three pompons on his front, shoe button eyes, and is jointed at the neck and arms. The value of the extremely rare teddy is $4,000.00+.

Pillow Bear stands 14" tall, with a gutta-percha nose. This type of nose was used on early teddy bears before noses were embroidered with floss or cord.

Strunz cat from 1910. This 6" tall beauty has an airbrushed velvet head and feet. The body is excelsior/kapok stuffed with a cotton velvet exterior. Stunning. $1,000.00+.

A rare example of the Strunz teddy bear from 1908 is shown here. Standing 11" tall, this teddy has perfect felt paw pads, shoe button eyes, and an exquisitely sewn nose. $1,800.00+.

Four distinctive cats and dogs. Sitting on the bench are the smallest Steiff Molly and Fluffy that were made in the 1930s. They are 2¼" tall, in great condition, and valued at $500.00 each. The little Steiff velvet dog in the front is from the 1920s and stands 3¾" tall. He is valued at $750.00+. The Strunz cat is also shown above.

American Greeting Cards has been featuring antique teddys from our collection on various cards, calendars, and gift bags since 1992. Here is an early Schuco gracing the front of a very special Valentine.

Chapter Five
Steiff Bears

What more could possibly be said about Steiff? It has maintained the highest degree of quality and acceptance since its inception over a century ago.

You can look at Steiff animals and bears in nearly every collectible book on plush animals. I have chosen some of our very special Steiff pieces that you have not seen before. The prices for mint and rare Steiff teddy bears are reaching ever higher.

As you enjoy looking through this chapter. perhaps it will bring pause to consider how very, very special your own treasures are. If you have one or more vintage Steiffs in your family, you do indeed own treasure.

This original photo is from a spot in Los Angeles, California. Dated January 11, 1908, the caption reads: "No sleigh bells for us." What a spectacular early American photo showing two great-looking children, two great teddy bears, a white Steiff on the porch, and an Ideal fabric-nosed bear on the car. There are also two dolls on the steps. Photo, $200.00.

Examine these photos closely, pictures of my 16" Steiff with that special horizontal-stitched nose.

I photographed this display which clearly shows a rare teddy bear by Steiff. Sitting on the block is a 16" Steiff dating from 1905. Although the card says it dates from 1903, I believe 1905 would be the earliest possible date. This bear is the only other one like this that I have ever heard of, and now I have seen it at the Smithsonian. The original nose on this bear is stitched horizontally, and the one I have from an original owner is also horizontally stitched. All other Steiffs that are 16" or taller have vertically stitched noses. The small bear in the photo is a 1907 Ideal teddy bear.

There are five sewn claws and a tiny pinhead-sized blank button in his ear. His condition is phenomenal!

A view from the back gives you an idea of this early bear's style. Nearly 100% kapok stuffed, he weighs almost nothing.

Sitting beside the Smithsonian picture, we can compare the twin bears. Now let us look at this bear in 1908, at 3 years old...with the original owner!

The bear in the buggy is the Steiff horizontal-sewn nose bear pictured previously. This bear is shown with the daughter of the State Attorney General and Supreme Court Justice from the state of Michigan. He bought this for her in 1905. She died at a young age, and I was offered the teddy some 90 years later. The value of this bear with provenance is too hard to assess. In our collection, it is invaluable.

A 1900 picture of the hardware store owned by the girl's grandfather, the very store from which the teddy bear and doll were purchased as gifts.

Original doll and teddy bear that have been companions since 1907. The doll is an Alabama doll, mint condition, and the bear is a blank button Steiff 13" from 1906.

An original photo of their owners, in 1907. Far to the side you can see the teddy bear, and in the little girl's lap we can see the doll.

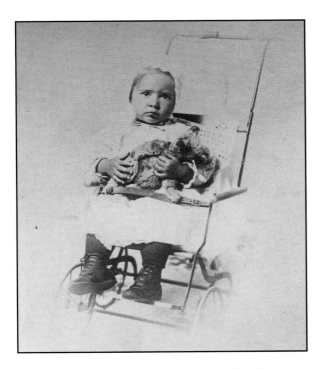

The same little girl in 1907 with her Steiff teddy bear.

Another little girl in 1912 with her Steiff teddy bear.

The 1907 Steiff teddy bear today!

What a great looking old Steiff, with photos of the original owner. Bear, $2,000.00+.

This rare 9" Steiff dates from 1908, and wears an original bloused shirt from that period. He is playing with a box of ladybugs, marked 25 cents each, from 1950. The little bear today is valued at $2,500.00+ and the ladybugs, $255.00 each.

The teddy at left is shown with his original owner in 1909. Actually the little girl is holding her little brother's Steiff bear, and the little boy is posing with his sister's doll…great picture.

Steiff's ability to capture the essence of an animal is something to behold. Standing in a birdbath, this 1912 King Charles Spaniel strikes a wonderful pose. With four jointed legs, a jointed head, push squeaker voice, and an early Steiff button, $2,000.00.

Two 1950s Steiff mohair birds have found the birdbath. Both of these expressive birds are in mint condition with chest tags and Steiff buttons on their tails. Hard to find, $300.00 each.

1907 was the year this Steiff 16" cinnamon teddy bear was created. He is playing with an original musical Black Forest carved bear from the same period. The marionette plays a tune as you hold it by the handle and twirl it round and round. It is valued at $750.00+. The 16" Steiff teddy is valued at $5,000.00+, especially with the photo of the owner.

Our 16" teddy from 1907 is seen being held by his original owner, wearing her navy dress.

Steiff from 1906 is shown with an original 11" bear in mint condition, and their replica with the chest tag shown. The replica is valued at $250.00, the original is valued at $2,500.00+.

The original photo of the 1906 11" Steiff. What a sweet photograph!

This Steiff is 13" tall and dates from 1907. I received him from the original owner, together with a heartwarming story. $4,000.00+.

Holding her kitty, this is the original owner of the 13" Steiff teddy. Although she had no photo with her teddy, the next best thing is this childhood photo with "thoughts about her childhood."

"You must have been a beautiful baby," and this is certainly a beautiful baby picture! Obtained from the original owner's son, this photo and the next two show three great items.

Dating from 1908, the owner's baby photo rests in the lap of his original Steiff 12" teddy bear. Observe the beautiful celluloid doll, which was also presented to the owner. The doll looks like it was hand done to resemble the photo.

The three items, all from the original owner. Set, $5,000.00+.

A summer scene from 1908 on a Victorian afternoon. The child's toys are both wheeled animals from that same year.

Although the bear in the Victorian photo is not available to show you, these next photos will show you similar Steiff bears. This 15" Steiff bear on wheels with a jointed "teddy" head from 1910 is a great-looking bear. With leather collar and chain, $2,500.00+.

Happy day! A 1909 photo of a real dog; a pair of white Steiff teddys; and a German AM doll. Photo, $50.00+.

Made of worsted wool, an early alternative to mohair, this Steiff measures 13" tall and dates from 1907. He has a jointed head, which is connected to metal rods instead of the cardboard discs which were used by this time for most teddy bears. In mint condition, $2,500.00+.

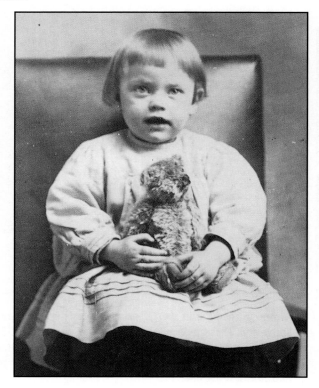

A 1907 photo of a child with her 12" Steiff. Photo, $40.00.

Steiff's little brown bear from 1910 is shown in this pre-WWI photograph. Photo, $40.00.

A 1910 Steiff teddy is rocked to sleep. Photo, $40.00.

A 1908 Steiff teddy is held by a real sweetheart. Photo, $50.00.

Standing behind the original photo with the owner is our 12" mint 1905 cinnamon Steiff. There is a blank button with remnants of a white tag in the ear. The side squeak voice works perfectly. With provenance, $5,000.00+.

A slightly different angle of the 1905 bear displays the deep color and extremely long arms. A treasure indeed.

Standing 14" tall, this teddy was displayed at Christmas from 1906 through 1912, and stored in a cedar chest until 1990 when I acquired him. This apricot/light cinnamon Steiff is "crispy mint." A perfect example, without one hair missing. With owner's provenance, $7,500.00+.

Enjoy this straight-on look, which helps detail the extremely thick, long pile of his mohair. This teddy is guessed as "new" by uninitiated collectors.

Steiff's 16" teddys from pre-1910 have a special personality. Enjoy the magnetic appeal of our wise old 16" teddy that we acquired from a antique market nearly two decades ago. At $750.00 he was the most expensive teddy around; today he is valued at $7,500.00.

Steiff cats are great. This six-way joint-ed cat was made around 1909. In excellent condition, $1,000.00.

A pair of antique sheep from 1912, in excellent condition. The one on the right is a Bing described earlier. The lamb on wheels is a splendid Steiff, standing 8" high and 12" long. The Steiff is valued at $1,500.00+.

Rare and white are the two points to bring home about this 10" white Steiff from 1920. In excellent condition, with button and squeaker, $2,500.00.

The white Steiff is seated outdoors beside a Nikki rabbit from the 1950s. In perfect condition, the rabbit is valued at $750.00+.

Teddy Babys are among our favorite style teddy. In *Teddy Bear Treasury* I you will see many versions, including the closed-mouth style. This one has a special countenance that simply makes you feel good. Standing 14" tall, 1930s, $3,000.00+.

A parting glance at one happy Teddy Baby.

Bears on all fours are sometimes equipped with jointed necks and teddy bear faces. This one is definitely a realistic bear by Steiff. Standing 6" tall and 9" long, the bear's golden mohair is as perfect as it was when new in 1914. This bear on wooden wheels, $2,000.00+.

A 4" tall 1930s King Charles Spaniel glances at Steiff's wool swan from 1950. The spaniel is valued at $1,000.00, and the swan at $125.00.

Dogs are favorites, even among teddy collectors. This is a 1920 black and white bully, and his companion is a 1950s miniature chow. Both stand about 4" tall and are valued at $750.00 for the bully, $250.00 for the chow.

Bully-bully! Getting a breath of fresh air, two bullys from the 1930s make a handsome pair. $750.00 for the small one, $1,500.00+ for the 8" tall one.

Pristine is the only word for this 8" tall Steiff bully, dating from 1930. $1,500.00+.

Another look at the pristine bully with a rare 8" white Steiff teddy from 1908. In excellent condition, the teddy is valued at $2,000.00+.

Allow me to introduce you to a 24" brown Steiff, made in the 1920s.

Sitting in his chair, his deep brown mohair contrasts noticeably with the lighter chair fabric.

Stepping outside, the bear's brown hues give way to cinnamon highlights.

Please notice the perfect condition of this original 1920s Steiff teddy.

Teddy's glance tells a life's story about to unfold.

This 1930 photo shows our brown Steiff in the arms of his original owner. This was taken in Germany, and the original owner is the father of the lady from whom I obtained the bear.

Jumping ahead some 20 years, this 1950s photo shows our brown Steiff in the arms of a friend of the owner who is sitting in the center.

Let us glance at a 1940s photo with our brown teddy's owner. This was taken in Austria. We also have the original leiderhosen worn by the teddy in this photo.

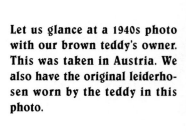

From about the same time period, a studio portrait shows our bear and the owner in a great pose.

An early 1940s snapshot from Germany shows the owner as a little girl, and the brown Steiff is sitting in the shadows. I was so fortunate receiving the bear, the photos, and most rewarding, the friendship of this teddy's owner. The brown 24" Steiff with its complete history documented is one of our favorite treasures. It is hard to put a monetary value on this particular teddy — to me it is priceless.

Have you experienced the lady bug explosion variety that we have in the Midwest? These are the most welcome breed that will ever fly into your home...Steiff wool lady bugs from 1950. Priced at 25 cents each when they were new, today the bugs solicit $25.00 each. The price is double that when you have a set in the original box as shown.

Wouldn't it be nice to have Steiff lady bugs swarm all over your house...just a thought.

In 20 years I have come in contact with only two of these special Steiff Zottys. What is so special about this one? He is a Zipper Zotty, in mint condition, with a chest tag and a zipper under his rear.

What a grand look he has, which adds to the value of this 1960 rarity. $1,500.00+.

Perfection is shown in this 11" Steiff Zotty. Sold through FAO Schwarz, he is in mint condition with a chest tag from Steiff and a wooden tag from Schwarz. $750.00+.

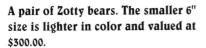

A pair of Zotty bears. The smaller 6" size is lighter in color and valued at $300.00.

Inside we get a better perspective of the coloration and detail of the 11" Zotty.

When we say mint, it means the tag or tags and air brushing are store new.

While we are talking about mint and hard to find, let us include the Steiff standing wolf. Dating from the 1950s, he is virtually unplayed-with. $1,500.00+

Personality plus best describes the little Steiff chow from the 1950s. The standing bear is the old Farnell shown earlier. In perfect condition, the chow is valued at $250.00.

Sitting for you, he displays the thick and rich mohair which covers him. These late 1940s and early 1950 versions are becoming more collectible every day.

This 20" Steiff is among their first post-WWII productions. In mint condition, with a wonderful growling voice, $2,000.00.

This beautiful Steiff cat is a hard to find early Diva, with an especially thick coat made from dralon. $250.00+.

The Toy Store in Toledo, Ohio, has provided us with years and years of collecting fun. Beth and Ben Savino at their annual Steiff Festival provide a challenge each year, to use their "theme" and create a vignette which will possibly be selected the "Best of Show." Brenda has won this honor four of the last five years, and the most recent winner is shown here. Using Steiff bluebirds and mice to help, our 1906 white 14" Steiff becomes Cinderella. The bluebirds are valued at $250.00 each, and the mice are $125.00 each. The 14" white Steiff teddy is valued at $7,500.00+.

(Top left) I thought you might enjoy a previous blue ribbon winner. Brenda used this 1920s globe and created the scene using an original 3½" teddy baby and an antique miniature tree and ladder. The Eskimo doll and polar bear look on.

(Top right) Shown with the recent prizes for "Best of Show" at the Steiff Festival in Toledo, Brenda is the deserving one. All I do is pick the bear to use, and she does the creating. Thanks again, Beth and Ben of the Toy Store – you bring out the best in us and many others.

(Left) American Greeting Cards has featured antique teddys from our collection for nearly 10 years. The two Steiffs featured in this sweetest day card are two of our favorites. Both are 20" tall, the girl dates from 1906, and the boy from 1907, and has a center seam. $8,000.00+ each.

Chapter Six

Friends & Their Bears

The greatest joy, according to President Theodore Roosevelt, "is to be in a room filled with your children, playing. It makes all other successes and achievements unimportant by comparison." He religiously set aside one hour each evening to play with his children. This was documented numerous times but certainly in the political book he handed out during his 1904 election campaign.

Thus began the "Century of the Child," as coined at the turn of the twentieth century. The varieties of playthings that survived this romantic period are the varied treasures we acknowledge here.

Teddy reigns supreme, as we begin another 100 years in which to celebrate a simple toy, made to bring joy. We give "A Salute to Teddy."

Repetition is indeed the mother of learning. Look, then look again at all the wonderful teddys and toys. Photographs are the primary identification source, and in time, anyone who is really interested in learning, will. Enjoy these photos sent from a few of our "teddy friends."

The Catherine "Sue" McKinney Collection

Catherine has a wonderful collection of dolls and teddy bears.

Take your time and pick out some of the special Schuco animals resting on these shelves. I spotted the yes-no panda in the cart on the top shelf, valued at $1,000.00+.

This unidentified teddy is shown with a picture of the original owner and the bear – great photo.

Did you want to see American teddy bears? Here are nine very special examples. All are pre-WWI and in excellent condition. $1,000.00 – 4,000.00 each.

Three 20" to 24" teddys in pristine condition. $2,000.00 – 3,000.00 each.

This original Ideal teddy from 1910 has the applied fabric nose and is in wonderful condition.

One of the early quality American teddys, this fellow has a stoic look. 20" tall, $2,000.00.

Cinnamon mohair is always desirable, and this is no exception. Ideal's WWI teddy is 16" tall. $1,000.00+.

Bing is one of Catherine's favorite makers, and she displays a Bing 24" teddy bear and doll, both from the 1920s. Value of this pair, with some wear, $4,000.00+.

Cramer's sweetest creation was little bearkin. Distributed through FAO Schwarz in the 1920s, he often had a suitcase and wardrobe.

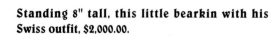

Standing 8" tall, this little bearkin with his Swiss outfit, $2,000.00.

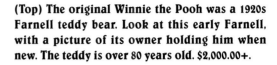

(Top) The original Winnie the Pooh was a 1920s Farnell teddy bear. Look at this early Farnell, with a picture of its owner holding him when new. The teddy is over 80 years old. $2,000.00+.

(Bottom left) One of the most prolific teddy bear makers who evolved from the Sonnenberg area, beginning in the early 1900s was Petz. This beautifully tipped teddy holds a surprise inside, a squeeze music box. Standing 16" tall, $3,000.00+.

(Bottom right) This is a German teddy baby design, but not a Steiff. 14" tall, $500.00.

An outdoors shot of this great Petz shows off the lighter tone of this musical gem.

Wilhelm Strunz was one of the earliest makers of teddy bears in Germany. This 15" teddy displays his gutta percha nose. Moderate thinning to the mohair, rare, $2,000.00.

This 19" beauty is one of the early Strunz rod bears. The thin rods are positioned similar to those in the Steiff rod bears except these are twisted and a bit thinner. The long straighter arms are typical of Strunz. $4,500.00+.

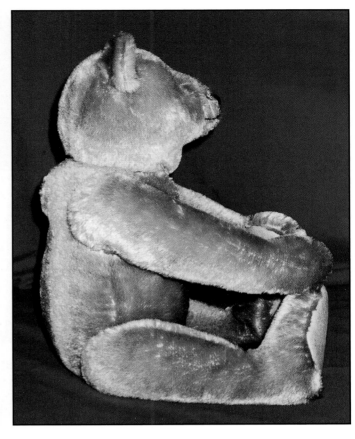

Dating from 1905, this rare Steiff is worth $10,000.00+.

At 20" this cone-shaped nose Steiff is among the very early production. Primarily kapok stuffed with a center seam in the head, the short thick pile mohair is rug quality.

Notice the close-up of the nose and center seam on this great specimen.

119

The 24" white Steiff is shown with an original photo of the bear and owner. Teddy with provenance, $15,000.00+.

Catherine's favorite, I believe, is her 24" white center seam Steiff. Here she sits, in all her glory.

Now this is a teddy bear. Showing a center seam and cinnamon brown mohair, this 1907 Steiff, 20" tall, is valued at $7,500.00+.

A 20" apricot Steiff from 1907 sits by a wonderful teddy bear drum. Teddy, $8,000.00+; drum, $400.00.

A trio of Steiff teddys, all early and wonderful.

(Top left) Standing 20" tall, this blond center seam Steiff is valued at $8,000.00+.

(Top right) Catherine's 24" 1910 Steiff teddy rests with his friend, a 1912 Steiff St. Bernard on wheels. Great looking pair. Dog, $1,200.00; teddy, $7,500.00+.

(Below) The 20" long nosed Steiff is valued at $7,500.00 and dates from 1908.

Although well worn, this 12" Steiff Dicky bear is a rare find. Dating from the 1920s, he is valued at $1,500.00+.

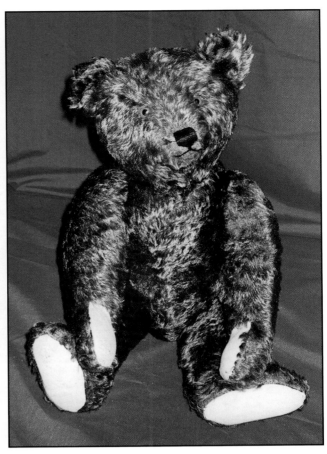

Dark brown teddy bears have a special realism, like this 20" Steiff from 1920. $5,000.00+.

Realism continues with these circa 1910 Steiff cats. All are six-way jointed, which includes the tail. $1,000.00 – 1,500.00 each.

Cats are also high on Catherine's collectible list, as shown by this beauty. This is one of the rarest and most special Schuco cats you will ever see, a yes-no from the 1920s. Near mint, $2,000.00+.

Certainly one of the finest Steiff realistic cats I have ever seen, dating from around 1910. $2,000.00.

Dating from the 1930s, this kitty is indeed hard to locate. Mint condition, $500.00.

Catherine's final photo shows two of her 1930s cats, one having the original kitty tag by Steiff. $500.00 each.

Pam and Charles are great collecting friends who appreciate the very special items. Appreciate this? A "filthy" St. Bernard on wheels, made by Steiff in 1913.

Brenda cleaned this diamond in the rough.

Magnificent 20" long Steiff. After cleaning, $2,000.00+.

A frontal view shows this dog's realism.

Steiff's 12" cinnamon brown teddy from 1909. $3,000.00+.

Received mint in this box, the Steiff teddy is 12 inches tall. He dates from 1906.

Getting a little fresh air, he displays his remarkable condition. $3,500.00+.

Very early blank button.

Teddy B and Teddy G? A white 1920s teddy and a cinnamon brown 1909. $3,000.00+ each.

A closer look at the white teddy details his excellent condition.

An array of mint Schuco miniature teddys from the 1950s. $250.00+ each.

A pair of early Steiffs, both 12" tall, $3,000.00 and $3,500.00.

Panda in a box...what a great collection. Each of these miniature pandas is worth $300.00+ and the box increases their total value. The little yes-no panda in front is worth $750.00+. The larger war zone 8" behind the box is valued at $1,500.00+.

Dressed Schuco boy and girl from 1948 are both 8" tall. The pair, $2,500.00+.

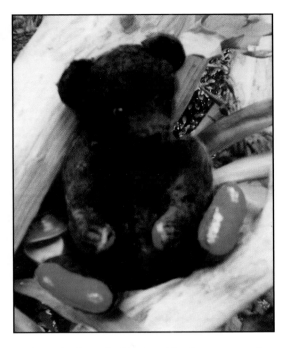

Our artist/collector friend from Down-Under sent me some excellent photos to share with you. This first one is my favorite, a rare black beauty. I am unable to certify the maker, but it is black mohair, with red felt pads. The shoe button eyes are backed with red felt circles. This could be a very valuable teddy bear, and it is magnificent to see.

A closer look at the black teddy shows a wonderful face and a horizontally stitched nose. The bear measures 14" tall. Great rare black teddy, probably from the 1910 – 1920 period.

The sweet look of the 1940 Chiltern is easy to recognize. This 16" charmer is valued at $300.00.

This Aussie bear is made by Lindee. Dating from around 1940 – 1950, the 18" tall teddy is valued at $350.00.

The glance of a 1940s Hermann teddy is shown here. 16" tall, he is valued at $300.00+.

A German Grisley from the 1950s in perfect condition. This 20" teddy is valued at $400.00.

Chad Valley produced these two friendly teddy bears around 1940. The large 20" is valued at $250.00 with his hair loss, while the smaller 15" is near perfect and valued at $500.00+.

An Australian favorite is this Joy Toy teddy produced 1920 – 1930. What an appealing personality. In excellent condition, $400.00.

This 16" Farnell dates from the 1920s when Christopher Robin played with a similar teddy. He does show a little hair loss, but then again, so do I and I am from the 1940s! $800.00.

The Phyllis Klein Collection

We are looking at a mint Steiff teddy from 1907. This 16" beauty is valued at $7,500.00+.

Dating from 1920, this 16" long-haired Bing is valued at $5,000.00+.

When you think of the ultimate Steiff antique teddy, the cinnamon-colored bear usually comes to mind. This 20" center seam example from 1907 is valued at $10,000.00+.

The most frequently found size of the old Steiff teddy bears is the 13" version from 1907. Even so, they are always a "must" for even the most advanced antique collector's shelf. This excellent example is valued at $4,000.00+.

Phyllis has a spectacular collection of silver "beara-phanalia." Every collection of teddy bears is enhanced with a least one of these early baby rattles. The items like these shown may range from $300.00 to $500.00. The teething ivory ringed rattle with a bell is marvelous.

What a gorgeous coat of antique white mohair. A West Highland terrier, dating from 1930, in near perfect condition. He has his Steiff button and red stock tag. A special pooch, valued at $1,500.00.

Buster Brown's Tige, dating from before 1910, sports a blank Steiff button on his ear, as well as the early leather leash. The dog is made of worsted wool with a mohair chest plate and paws. Very expressive example. $1,000.00+.

Nancy's sweet Chiltern always appears wanting to be held. At 20" tall, this early 1920 – 1930 example is truly a "Hug me bear." Collectors pay up to $1,000.00 for one this special.

Schuco made Trippel-Trappel walking dogs in many breeds. One of the hardest to find is the Westie, which dates from 1948, and is in mint condition. $500.00+.

Popular 1960s cats in mint condition are Susi, Tapsy, and Gussy. $200.00+ each.

A trio of Steiff cats from around 1960, two Kittys, and one sleep-eyed Snurry. $150.00+ each.

Nancy's very own childhood Knickerbocker dating from 1935, her playpal and personal pet. In wonderful condition with provenance, $500.00+.

This trio of hard to find puppies all date from different decades. The sitting Westie is a Steiff from the 1930s and valued at $750.00+. The Black Scotty is an unnamed German mechanical with a wooden knob under the torso which allows you to rotate the head. This Scotty is from around 1940 and is valued at $500.00. The Dalmatian is a Steiff from the 1950s, in perfect condition, $500.00.

White mohair attracts attention...and collectors. A beautiful 10" 1905 Steiff, with a blank button, will bring $2,500.00+ from collectors. Great teddy!

Farnell made truly special animals as shown by this early fox. Dating pre-WWII, this is a musical fox with a tag that reads. "Alpha Farnell, music: A hunting we will go." $750.00+.

Standing 17" tall, a 1940s yes-no Schuco teddy is as perfect as he was over 50 years ago. He is valued at $2,000.00+ today.

American Ideal Toy and Novelty teddy from 1907, splendid in every respect. 24" tall, featuring a stately stature, in pristine condition. $3,000.00+.

A view of just a part of Nancy's miniature pound. These dogs date from around 1950, with at least one terrier in the center from the 1920s. These puppies range from $125.00 to $500.00, depending on the rarity of the breed.

The Sandy DeRhodes Collection

Sandy has provided a few examples of the "before" and "after" looks of several vintage teddy bears. She is a collector and lover of teddys first and that makes her even better at her repair effort.

Before and after cleaning and restoration, a 1920s Petz clown styled teddy. This refurbished 16" example after the work, $1,000.00.

The American Hecla bear is a sought-after teddy. Among the first made in 1906 or 1907, this example was in great need of Sandy's attention. The original shoe buttons were put back in, and the temporary red glass eyes removed. A properly sewn nose and the old leather covering removed from the feet revealed the originals in good condition. The finished teddy, $1,000.00+.

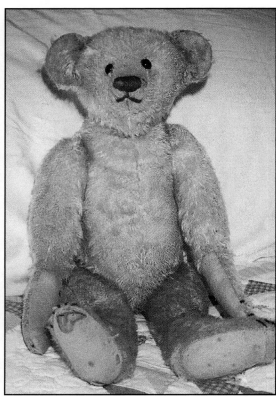

A German Petz teddy, 20" tall, before and after. What a dramatic difference when the bear is properly cleaned, padded, and stuffed. Refinished Petz, $600.00.

Over time, some teddys are given over-sewn noses, as well as foot and hand pads. This 1907 Hecla was cleaned properly, and the over-sewn items removed. Sandy's restored Hecla is worth in excess of $1,000.00.

Early Strauss teddy bears are very difficult to find. This American Strauss stands 16" tall but sits proudly after Sandy gave him his first bath in 90 years. $1,500.00+.

Ideal Toy and Novelty is noted by many as the first American manufacturer of teddy bears. A white Ideal is highly prized, especially when it has the sweet look of this guy. Sandy had to replace the ears and restitch the nose, as well as properly clean this 16" gem. After all is said and done, this beauty is valued at $750.00 – $1,000.00.

~

Another Hecla? She has hit the jackpot, with another beauty. At 16" tall, the "after" teddy is valued at $1,000.00. Nice work, Sandy.

~

A magnificent 24" Steiff teddy from 1920. He has gray-brown tipped mohair and a wonderfully "wise" grin. In exceptional condition, aside from some thinning of his long pile mohair, he is valued at $7,500.00+.

Every advanced collector wants to own a Steiff center seam bear. My favorite size is the 16" version, as shown here. Dating from 1908, in perfect condition with a working growler, this marvelous teddy is valued at $10,000.00+.

Standing 20" tall, dating from 1907, and in near mint condition, this Steiff teddy possesses a natural smile. I know he makes Michelle happy! The value of this more common color is $8,000.00+.

Since the earliest teddy bears, white mohair has had a profoundly positive effect on a bear's desirability. This 24" version is a very early 1905 – 1906 example, making him very rare indeed. His value is well over $10,000.00.

A 20" Steiff teddy with a working growler dating from 1908 is very sought after. Add to these characteristics the coat of white mohair, and the sky is the limit on demand. This wonderful teddy is worth well over $10,000.00.

From Michelle's vast collection, she has included one of her early American bears. This pristine example dates from 1910, and is 24" tall. The simplicity of his style is what draws many bear lovers to this kind of teddy. In perfect condition, $3,000.00.

What a great Steiff teddy bear from 1907! Nearly 95 years old, this 18" beauty is in excellent condition, with the desired center seam. $10,000.00+.

A quizzical glance from Michele's 18" center seam teddy.

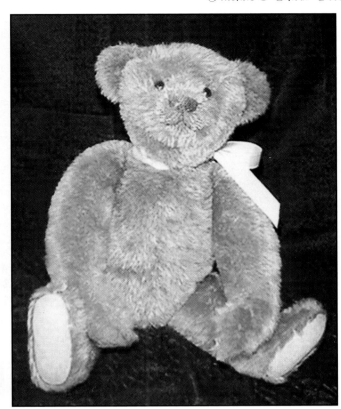

Dating from 1905, this 13" Steiff has the "real teddy" face. $4,000.00.

Cinnamon remains one of, if not the most sought after color by antique teddy bear collectors. At 13" tall, dating from 1907, this Steiff cinnamon teddy commands attention. $5,000.00+.

A dynamic duo of Steiff teddys poses for us. At 10" and 13", they are both highly valued by teddy collectors. The 10" is valued at $3,000.00. The 13" white Steiff is valued at $5,000.00+.

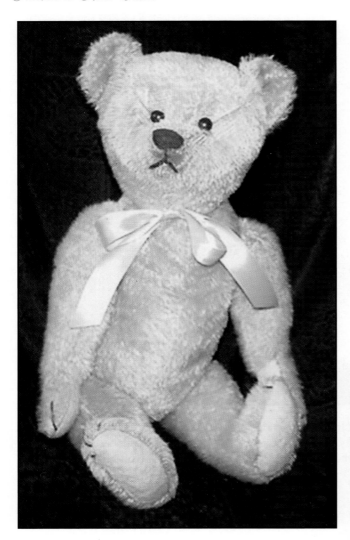

A sweet faced 18" American teddy dating from 1908. Probably Ideal Toy and Novelty Co. In excellent condition, $2,000.00.

Strunz is a very rare old bear to find, and this 25" example is splendid. Dating from 1907, he is a marvelous example of early German teddy bear making. $5,000.00.

Dating from 1910, this German Petz teddy has the typical "sliced-in ears" as introduced by this company in 1906-1907. A wonderful mint 14" example. $2,000.00.

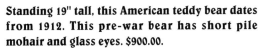

Standing 19" tall, this American teddy bear dates from 1912. This pre-war bear has short pile mohair and glass eyes. $900.00.

An early Ideal teddy bear with leather recovered pads, in wonderful condition. At 12" tall, this little teddy is valued at $750.00.

From Our Family

Throughout our collecting years, Brenda and I have always been interested in learning about the original owners of the teddy bears we find. I thought it appropiate to bring *Teddy Bear Treasury* II to a special conclusion. Brenda's mother and Brenda's sister's father-in-law are shown below, many years ago with their childhood teddy bears.

What a great photo! Dating from the "Roaring 20s," this photo captures a group of friends gathered for a theme party. They were each asked to bring their favorite childhood toy, and notice the one person who did not bring a doll! That is Alberta G. Brandfass, Brenda's mom, holding her 1909 Ideal teddy bear. Alberta is 92 years young today and still loves teddy bears.

Alberta G. Brandfass today!

Dwight M. Brown, Brenda's sister's father-in-law, with
his childhood bear in 1909, a 1906 Steiff teddy.

Ninety-five-year-old Dwight M. Brown today,
holding his son's Knickerbocker teddy.

Chapter Seven
Photo Finish

There are many teddys that are looking forward to their appearance in *Teddy Bear Treasury* III. These final photos are some of them that just would not wait for the next book.

Our good friend Jim Buckey is responsible for making the French drumming bear (pg. 71) tap out a rhythm again.

Jim performed open-heart surgery on this 125-year-old French clockwork toy. Thanks again, Jim…rat-a-tat-tat!

A teddy does not have to be mint to be precious. This is a 12" Steiff Petsy from the 1920s. Sweet blue eyes, thinned tipped mohair, and a center head seam help create one of our most precious looking teddy bears. Value is less than $1,000.00 in worn condition.

What big ears you have! That was my first comment when I found him. As I reached to touch the ears, I found working squeakers in each one!

Notice the long luxurious mohair and small torso, yet long thick arms and legs. This rare teddy was traced to an English maker, around 1914. Peacock is the probable maker. In mint condition, $3,000.00.

151

Teddy dressed as a Rough Rider was made around 1910 by the American Stuffed Toy Company. All original, with a "Won't you be my Teddy Bear" button on his shirt, he stands 24" tall. Uniquely dressed, his body is made of cloth, and mohair is used only for the extremities. Rare and very desirable, his value is $2,000.00+.

This 20" Ideal teddy bear dates from 1907, and is purported to be one of the first made at the factory which opened in January of that year. All original, and in near mint condition, he is valued at $7,500.00+.

Study his profile, it is seldom seen in such glorious condition. The shoe button eyes are set just inside the head seam, one of the traits of the Ideal teddy bears.

A close-up of this magnificent Ideal shows the great detail used in their earliest teddys.

Ideal teddy bears from 1908 looked like this when they were brand new!

Dating from exactly 1908, we can observe the slight change that occurred between the 1907 bear and the one shown here. This bear stands 19" tall and is in mint condition. Value as shown is $5,000.00+.

A few friendly teddys decided to pose on this first day of spring.

Left to right: 24" American Stuffed Toy Company's Rough Rider, from 1910; 12" Steiff Petsy from 1928; 19" Ideal Toy & Novelty Co., 1908; 12" Steiff Teddy Baby, with closed mouth, 1928; 20" Ideal Toy & Novelty Co., 1907; (seated) 13" Heinrich Silberstein, 1907 (velvet nose and pads); 16" Gerbruder Bing from 1914, dark cinnamon mohair, mint; (in front) 6" Gerbruder Bing from 1907, rare miniature, mint; 20" Steiff Teddy "White" from 1914.

What else can you say, teddy says it all. Dating from 1912 – 1920, this 20" white Steiff is in mint condition. Value is in the $10,000 range.

A close-up of teddy's face shows us how artistically perfect a teddy can be.

Evaluation Certificate

When buying or selling a vintage teddy bear, we trust it is indeed what we think it to be.

Fortunately, reputable dealers and shop owners abound. If you have access to one of these special people, utilize that trust, and have them validate your "treasures."

You may have an old teddy, or related collectible that you have no intention of ever selling. Still, you should know the market value, in case you would want it insured. If you are selling an item, you deserve a price commensurate with the value. I have done countless evaluations for GBW, libraries, museums, senior citizen clubs, teddy bear shops, hospitals, and various fund raisers. One item I consider very important to have issued is an evaluation certificate.

For your personal item I will provide a free evaluation certificate. Simply copy the form on this page, and send it to me at Ken Yenke, P.O. Box 361633, Strongsville, Ohio 44136, with a self-addressed stamped return envelope and a photograph and description of your teddy. I will provide you with a complete evaluation of your item, using my best effort. We will allow one free evaluation with each book purchased. If you have more items in need of evaluation, a nominal fee can be arranged.

Once you get your evaluation certificate, you should store it safely, with a photo of your item. This provides a validation should you ever be required to prove your ownership.

EVALUATION CERTIFICATE

Probable Manufacturer:

Approximate Age:

Current Market Value (Range):

Special Comments Regarding This Item:

Date of Evaluation:

For: _____   By: _____

Note: The above evaluation is intended as a guide to your knowledge of the item. I cannot be responsible for profits or losses involving the sale or disposal of this item.

COLLECTOR BOOKS

Informing Today's Collector

For over two decades we have been keeping collectors informed on trends and values in all fields of antiques and collectibles.

BOOKS ON DOLLS —

4631	**Barbie Doll** Boom, 1986–1995, Augustyniak	$18.95
2079	**Barbie Doll Fashion**, Vol. I, Eames	$24.95
4846	**Barbie Doll Fashion**, Vol. II, 1968–1974, Eames	$24.95
5672	The **Barbie Doll** Years, 4th. Ed., Olds	$19.95
3957	**Barbie Exclusives**, Rana	$18.95
4632	**Barbie Exclusives**, Book II, Rana	$18.95
5352	**Barbie Doll Exclusives** & More, 2nd Ed. Augustyniak	$24.95
5155	Collector's Ency. of **American Composition Dolls**, Mertz	$24.95
2211	Collector's Ency. of **Madame Alexander Dolls**, Smith	$24.95
4863	Collector's Encyclopedia of **Vogue Dolls**, Izen/Stover	$29.95
5148	Collector's Guide to **Barbie Doll Vinyl Cases**, Kaplan	$12.95
5160	Collector's Guide to **Ideal Dolls**, 2nd Edition, Izen	$24.95
4707	Decade of **Barbie Dolls** & Collectibles, 1981–1991, Summers	$19.95
5821	**Doll Values**, Antique to Modern, 5th Ed., Moyer	$12.95
5599	**Dolls of the 1960s and 1970s**, Sabulis	$24.95
1799	**Effanbee Doll** Encyclopedia, Smith	$19.95
5829	**Madame Alexander** Price Guide #26, Crowsey	$12.95
5611	**Madame Alexander** Store Exclusives & Ltd. Eds., Crowsey	$24.95
5050	**Modern Collectible Dolls**, Volume II, Moyer	$19.95
5269	**Modern Collectible Dolls**, Volume III, Moyer	$24.95
5612	**Modern Collectible Dolls**, Volume IV, Moyer	$24.95
5833	**Modern Collectible Dolls**, Volume V, Moyer	$24.95
5689	**Nippon Dolls** & Playthings, Van Patten/Lau	$29.95
5059	**Skipper**, Barbie Doll's Little Sister, Arend/Holzerland/Kent	$19.95
5253	Story of **Barbie**, 2nd Ed., Westenhouser	$24.95
1817	**Teddy Bears & Steiff Animals**, 2nd Series, Mandel	$19.95
2084	**Teddy Bears & Steiff Animals**, 3rd Series, Mandel	$19.95
5371	**Teddy Bear** Treasury, Yenke	$19.95
5049	Thirty Years of **Mattel Fashion Dolls**, Augustyniak	$19.95
1808	Wonder of **Barbie**, Manos	$9.95
4880	The World of **Raggedy Ann** Collectibles, Avery	$24.95
1430	World of **Barbie** Dolls, Manos	$9.95

BOOKS ON TOYS, MARBLES & CHRISTMAS COLLECTIBLES —

2333	Antique & Collectible **Marbles**, 3rd Ed., Grist	$9.95
5607	Antiquing and Collecting on the **Internet**, Parry	$12.95
5353	**Breyer Animal** Collector's Guide, 2nd Ed., Browell	$19.95
5608	Buying, Selling & Trading on the **Internet**, 2nd Ed., Hix	$12.95
5150	**Cartoon Toys** & Collectibles, Longest	$19.95
4976	**Christmas Ornaments**, Lights & Decorations, Johnson	$24.95
4737	**Christmas Ornaments**, Lights & Decorations, Vol. II	$24.95
4739	**Christmas Ornaments**, Lights & Decorations, Vol. III,	$24.95
4559	Collectible **Action Figures**, 2nd Ed., Manos	$17.95
2338	Collector's Encyclopedia of **Disneyana**, Longest/Stern	$24.95
5149	Collector's Guide to **Bubble Bath Containers**, Moore/Pizzo	$19.95
5038	Coll. Gde. to **Diecast Toys** & Scale Models, 2nd Ed., Johnson	$19.95
5681	Collector's Guide to **Lunchboxes**, White	19.95
5621	Collector's Guide to **Online Auctions**, Hix	$12.95
5169	Collector's Guide to **T.V. Toys** & Memorabilia, Davis/Morgan	$24.95
4651	Collector's Guide to **Tinker Toys**, Strange	$18.95
4566	Collector's Guide to **Tootsietoys**, 2nd Ed., Richter	$19.95
5360	**Fisher-Price Toys**, Cassity	$19.95
4945	**G-Men & FBI Toys** & Collectibles, Whitworth	$18.95
4720	Golden Age of **Automotive Toys**, Hutchison/Johnson	$24.95
5593	Grist's Big Book of **Marbles**, 2nd Ed.	$24.95
3970	Grist's Machine-Made & Contemporary **Marbles**, 2nd Ed.	$9.95
5684	Hake's Price Guide to **Character Toys**, 3rd Edition	$35.00
5267	**Matchbox Toys**, 3rd Ed., 1947 to 1998, Johnson	$19.95
5830	**McDonald's** Collectibles, 2nd Edition, Henriques/DuVall	$24.95
5673	Modern **Candy Containers** & Novelties, Brush/Miller	$19.95
1540	Modern **Toys**, 1930–1980, Baker	$19.95
3888	**Motorcycle Toys**, Antique & Contemporary, Gentry/Downs	$18.95
5365	**Peanuts Collectibles**, Podley/Bang	$24.95
5693	Schroeder's Collectible **Toys**, Antique to Modern, 7th Ed.	$17.95
5277	**Talking Toys** of the 20th Century, Lewis	$15.95

Schroeder's
ANTIQUES
Price Guide

OUR
#1
BEST-
SELLER!

...is the #1 bestselling antiques & collectibles value guide on the market today, and here's why...

• *More than 450 advisors, well-known dealers, and top-notch collectors work together with our editors to bring you accurate information regarding pricing and identification.*

• *More than 50,000 items in over 600 categories are listed along with hundreds of sharp original photos that illustrate not only the rare and unusual, but the common, popular collectibles as well.*

• *Each large close-up shot shows important details clearly. Every subject is represented with histories and background information, a feature not found in any of our competitors' publications.*

• *Our editors keep abreast of newly developing trends, often adding several new categories a year as the need arises.*

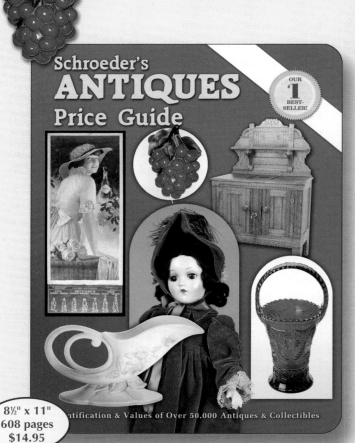

Schroeder's
ANTIQUES
Price Guide

OUR
#1
BEST-
SELLER!

Identification & Values of Over 50,000 Antiques & Collectibles

8½" x 11"
608 pages
$14.95

If it merits the interest of today's collector, you'll find it in *Schroeder's*. And you can feel confident that the information we publish is up-to-date and accurate. Our advisors thoroughly check each category to spot inconsistencies, listings that may not be entirely reflective of market dealings, and lines too vague to be of merit. Only the best of the lot remains for publication.

cb

COLLECTOR BOOKS
P.O. Box 3009 • Paducah, KY 42002–3009
www.collectorbooks.com

Without doubt, you'll find
Schroeder's Antiques
Price Guide
the only one to buy for
reliable information
and values.